Daughter
ARISE!

Daughter
ARISE!

Defy Your Limitations
and Scale the Utmost Height

Fatima Sibanda

SIBANDA
PUBLISHING

A catalogue record for this book is available from the British Library.

Published in the United Kingdom by Sibanda Publishing.

ISBN: 978-0-9561175-4-0

Dedication

This book is dedicated to my two lovely daughters,
Ayanda and Realeboga.
May the Lord help you to scale the utmost height
that He has planned for you.

Lord Plant My Feet On Higher Ground

I'm pressing on the upward way,
New heights I'm gaining every day;
Still praying as I'm onward bound,
"Lord, plant my feet on higher ground."

Refrain:
Lord, lift me up and let me stand,
By faith, on Heaven's tableland,
A higher plane than I have found;
Lord, plant my feet on higher ground.

My heart has no desire to stay
Where doubts arise and fears dismay;
Though some may dwell where those abound,
My prayer, my aim, is higher ground.

I want to live above the world,
Though Satan's darts at me are hurled;
For faith has caught the joyful sound,
The song of saints on higher ground.

I want to scale the utmost height
And catch a gleam of glory bright;
But still I'll pray till heav'n I've found
"Lord, plant my feet on higher ground."

Johnson Oatman Jr. (1856-1922)

A Word from the Author

The Bible has many accounts of women who could not maximise their potential due to limiting conditions placed on them by various circumstances beyond their control.

It is worth noting that the limitations that women faced in the centuries past are still rearing their ugly heads at today's woman! Sadly, millions of women around the world are still operating below their capacity. Many have already populated graveyards without having had a chance to live their dreams or to do the things they were born for. They had a story to tell that could have benefited society, but their circumstances put a zip on their lips.

Cultural and traditional barriers have dictated to thousands of women how far they can go in life. Lines of limitation have been drawn in various spheres with clear instructions, "Thou shalt not cross", and if they dare to cross, it's at their own risk!

A friend told me that in the country in which they have been working as expatriates, women are not allowed to drive! That is a privilege for men and their teenage sons. Young boys can drive their mothers around but, "Mother, you shall not touch the steering wheel for the day you touch it, you shall surely be arrested!" So should there be no son who can drive, and an emergency happens and dad is not there, they will not be able to go and get help. Whatever the rationale behind this law is, the fact remains that it is an institutionalised limitation placed on women and girls.

Women's abilities have been questioned and many assumptions have been made as to what they can and cannot do. Unfortunately, even within my field, which is the church some denominations do not allow women to be ministers or occupy senior positions such as bishops. In some cases, they are expected to operate under their husbands' name.

Some churches do not even allow women to preach. Ironically, the work of the ministry or pastoral work is supposed to be led by the Holy Spirit, who is genderless. The work of regeneration and transformation of the heart is done by the Word and the Spirit of God. I wonder if the human heart only responds to the Word of God if it's taught by male teachers?

Others argue that women can teach but can't pastor. How come the secular world has female managers and directors of companies? Why not within the church setting? Many church organisations have given the excuse that Jesus had twelve male apostles. How about Anna the prophetess, who waited for the birth of Jesus in the Temple, praying day and night?

Some remind us that the Apostle Paul said that women should not teach, but that was Paul's world and culture of the day. Are those the days we live in? What is the real reason behind this? Is this not just one of the many unjustified limitations placed on women? Despite all the excuses and reasons given for placing limitations on women, with God's help, many have risen up and impacted their world.

This book is a call to women to rise up and refuse to bow to any limitations. You have what it takes to make a difference in your life and the lives around you. You have the power to influence positively and to contribute to your generation. It's time to move to a higher level of effectiveness. It's time to expand; God is able to remove any ceiling that wants to stop you. Daughter of the Most High God, arise! It's time to stand up and be counted! Rise up and do the things you were born for. Live your dream, for the Lord is with you. Arise and bless the world around you with the love of God, with your gifts, abilities, time and skills. Arise, because you are a gift to this world and the Lord is with you.

Daughter, rise up and scale the utmost height!

Contents

Chapter One
Hannah's Story

A limitation can be defined as a restricting condition, an inability, a disadvantage, a drawback, an impediment, an inhibition, a prohibition or a constraint. With this in mind, let us explore the life of an amazing woman whose story is found in the book of *I Samuel chapters 1–3.*

Hannah was married to Elkanah and she shared her husband with Peninnah, who was his other wife. This was a great limitation for Hannah as you can probably imagine. Just think of how you would feel being married to a man who could never fully be yours because he had another woman in his life to look after! He would constantly have to divide his love and affection between both of you. You might desire to be with him at a moment when he is with the other woman, so you would have to wait for your turn. This would limit what you could do together as there would always be 'the other' person in the relationship that you would have to consider. She might also feel the same way about you! And no matter how much he may try to please you both equally, it would be impossible. This is because a man was originally designed to be married to one woman for one lifetime, not two!

Hannah had to contend with this predicament in her life. The scriptures do not state whether she was Elkanah's first or second wife, but they do indicate that it didn't seem to be her primary concern. What was more of a pressing issue to Hannah was her barrenness. *I Samuel 1:2b* says that, *"Peninnah had children, but Hannah had no children" (ESV).* Failing to bear children was Hannah's major limitation. And what made matters worse was that her counterpart Peninnah, had five children.

I'm sure that it was very painful for Hannah to watch each and every one of Peninnah's pregnancies while not having any children of her own. If each of Peninnah's children were weaned after two years, then Hannah's 'pregnancy-bump-watching' experience lasted for approximately ten years! I doubt that Hannah was such an angel that she didn't feel a pinch of envy, wishing that just one of those pregnancies were hers. She was human and perhaps in her little heart she might have even wished that Peninnah would miscarry so that she didn't feel so miserable. It didn't seem fair that Peninnah seemed to be the 'chosen one' to bear all of Elkanah's children. Furthermore, Peninnah was not at all sympathetic towards Hannah.

Whilst the Bible mentions that Elkanah loved Hannah, it doesn't mention that he loved Peninnah. It appears that their case was similar to that of Rachel and Leah. Although Jacob's true love was Rachel. Leah was the one having most of Jacob's children. Both Rachel and Hannah were loved more by their husbands than their counterparts and yet they were unable to conceive, while the unloved wives were the ones birthing all the babies.

Perhaps being the unloved wife in Peninnah's case could explain her nastiness to Hannah. *1 Samuel 1:6* says *"her rival would make fun of her mercilessly, just to bother her"* (*CEB*). *Verse 7* says *"her rival provoked her till she wept and would not eat"* (*NIV*). In today's terminology, Hannah experienced verbal and psychological bullying from Peninnah. This is a form of abuse. It's one thing to be barren, but it's quite another to be laughed at because of it. In her ridicule and jeering of Hannah, Peninnah was rubbing salt into a gaping wound. Barrenness was not something that Hannah could change and not only was her limitation affecting her emotionally; the mistreatment she endured from Peninnah caused her to lose her appetite. It appears that Hannah was somewhat depressed, and understandably so. The Bible doesn't say how long she didn't eat, but it was long enough to be recorded. In ministering to women who have been through similar situations, I have noticed that eating disorders are quite common due to emotional trauma or stress.

As if this wasn't already enough for Hannah, yearly sacrifices to the Lord as required by law, were another bitter reminder of her inadequacy and limitation. It was that time of the year again and Elkanah dished out portions of meat for Peninnah and her sons to sacrifice, and in comparison Hannah only got a small portion of meat for herself. Some translations say Elkanah gave her two portions or a 'choice' portion because he loved her, but her husband's love did not change the fact that she was barren. Hannah wept and Elkanah tried to console her by saying, *"Hannah, why are you weeping? Why don't you eat? Why are you downhearted? Don't I mean more to you than ten sons?" (Verse 8, NIV)*. But Hannah knew very well the difference between a husband and a son, and she wanted a son. Although Elkanah was attempting to help her, his response seemed to be quite insensitive.

Hannah had been going to Shiloh to offer sacrifices yearly, but this time it was different. In verse 10 it says that Hannah was "deeply distressed". She just couldn't take it any more and so she *"prayed to the Lord and wept bitterly" (ESV)*. She decided to pour out her heavily-laden heart to the Lord. It had been carrying years of disappointment, hurt and pain. Peninnah's continuous show off contributed to Hannah feeling rejected. Rejection is like a deadly poison, it kills. It has been observed that rejection stems from feelings of being unwanted and unaccepted. It often results in approval addictions, resentment, bitterness, insecurity, jealousy, competition, anger, fear, suspicion, poor self-image, stubbornness, self-pity, self-preservation, amongst many other off-shoots. Hannah must have developed some of these in her heart. She had experienced piercing emotional pain, resulting in her deep distress.

Her desperation overflowed. She prayed until she could no longer utter any more words. As her heart drained of all its anguish, her body must have been shaking. Eli the priest saw her lips moving but didn't hear her voice and this perplexed him. He assumed that Hannah was drunk and in verse 14 he asked her, "How long are you going to stay drunk? Put away your wine."

I have to admire how Hannah handled Eli's accusation. If she hadn't been in the presence of the Lord, perhaps she would have responded very differently to Eli! She's childless, she's being made fun of, her husband thinks he's enough for her, and finally when she is desperately praying, the priest accuses her of being drunk! This might have been the last straw. She could have said, "That's it, I am out of here!" or at that moment she could have stopped praying and given Eli such a telling off that he would have regretted ever opening his mouth! Rather Hannah graciously explained her situation: *"Not so, my lord,"* she replied, *"I am a woman who is deeply troubled. I have not been drinking wine or beer; I was pouring out my soul to the Lord. Do not take your servant for a wicked woman; I have been praying here out of my great anguish and grief."*

Hannah's response showed that she was not distracted by Eli's thoughtless remark because she knew who she was pouring out her soul to. She had enough of being the victim and cried out for deliverance. She was no longer focussing on Peninnah, Elkanah, Eli or even her barrenness! Her eyes were now on Yahweh, her Maker, and the giver of life. It was through prayer that she pushed past her limitations and evoked the supernatural. Her breakthrough was imminent. Eli responded to Hannah by saying, *"Go in peace, and may the God of Israel grant you what you have asked of him"* (verse 17).

Hannah did not leave the place of prayer before emptying her whole heart before the Lord. Neither did she go back home empty-handed. Verse 18 states that she "went her way and ate, and her face was no longer sad." Although her miracle was not yet manifest, her sorrow had been traded for joy, her ashes for beauty, and her garment of heaviness had been replaced with a garment of praise. A woman, who because of tremendous turmoil could not face eating food, now had her appetite restored!

Things permanently shifted for Hannah and in *verse 20* we learn that God answered her prayer. *"Hannah conceived and bore a son, and she called his name Samuel, for she said, 'I have asked for him from the Lord'"* (ESV). Hannah promised the Lord that her son would be given back to Him, and after weaning him, she kept her promise and presented him to the Lord. Samuel grew up and served in the temple. He became the great prophet of Israel — the very prophet who anointed David as king of Israel.

Beyond Hannah's limitation lay Samuel. If she had succumbed to her condition and accepted her barrenness as her lot in life, Israel would have been deprived of receiving instructions and guidance from the Lord. Samuel would never have been born and Penninah may have continued to harass Hannah. Who knows what would have become of her? Perhaps we would be reading a very different story in the Bible. But Hannah was determined. In spite of her intense sorrow, she still prayed. She still cried to God even when there were no more words to utter. For a while Penninah seemed to have a higher advantage over Hannah, but God levelled the ground. No longer could she torment Hannah for being barren. They were now equally mothers, regardless of how many children they had. Yahweh had the final say.

Like Hannah, you need to get fed up with your current situation. If you don't, you won't move on with your life. Regardless of what you have been through, connect with the heavens in prayer. Empty out your heart to the Maker of hearts and give God complete access. Don't hide anything from Him, but be real with yourself and with Him. Allow Him to work in your life and remove the residue from past hurts and disappointments. Let Him lift you above the Peninnahs and Elis of this world. Don't allow your limitations to stop you. You are the daughter of the Most High. It's time to rise up and defy your limitations!

Chapter One

Reflect, Pray and Apply

💬 Reflection points

- What are your current limitations?

- What aspects of Hannah's life do you identify with?

- Do you still have issues that need to be dealt with before the Lord?

🤍 Practical steps to take

1. Find a quiet place and search your heart.

2. Honestly evaluate where you are at.

3. Pray and ask the Lord to help you deal with issues.

4. Repent if you find areas in which you responded wrongly to negative circumstances.

5. Pray for those who might have hurt you and let go of any rejection – it is a deadly poison!

6. Forgiveness is a ticket to your own freedom. You can't afford not to forgive.

📖 Scripture Focus

Psalm 121:1-8 (*KJV*)

"I will lift up mine eyes unto the hills, from whence cometh my help. My help cometh from the Lord, which made heaven and earth. He will not suffer thy foot to be moved: he that keepeth thee will not slumber. Behold, he that keepeth Israel shall neither slumber nor sleep. The Lord is thy keeper: the Lord is thy shade upon thy right hand. The sun shall not smite thee by day nor the moon by night. The Lord shall preserve thee from all evil: he shall preserve thy soul. The Lord shall preserve thy going out and thy coming in from this time forth and even for evermore."

Beloved, rest assured that the Lord is going to help you.

Chapter Two
My Story

One of the defining moments of my life was my wedding day. Months prior to the day were filled with great excitement and preparations. The bridal party would meet regularly to rehearse their dance steps. The dresses for the bridesmaids were chosen, and so were the groomsmen's suits, rings and everything that goes with it, all was in order. Finally, the great day arrived. It was a big wedding and the church service was packed. People sang, danced, laughed and cried to witness such an event. The presence of the Lord was tangible as I walked down the aisle to a song my sister Tracy was singing. The words were based on *Psalm 34:3: "O magnify the Lord with me, and let us exalt His name together" (KJV)*. My in-laws were ululating, shouting praises and words of welcoming me into their family. My family were beaming with joy. My mum was thrilled as she received a new son! Being the proud mother of the bride, she was excited to see me gracefully take such a major step. It was surely a great day. When the ceremony was over, pastors gathered around us and prayed for God's blessing on our marriage. They also prayed that we would be blessed with godly children and that only death would separate Osie and I.

After all the hustle and bustle of the wedding we took off for our honeymoon at the Victoria Falls — one of the Seven Natural Wonders of the World. The moon was there but I don't remember the honey (the honeymoon!) as a first-time bride, but overall our time there was indescribably precious. As we cruised on the Zambezi River we fantasized about different things, including how many children we would have and what sort of life we wanted to live. All was fabulous!

Three months later we were in Botswana with friends, having fun. As newlyweds, we were travelling a lot, and at that time my husband was a lay preacher and was involved with planting churches in different parts of Botswana. One evening, I started feeling nauseous and I had no clue what caused it . The feeling worsened, and by then we were in Zimbabwe. We went to see a doctor, and a scan was booked because I could now see traces of blood in my urine. The following week I was in theatre. They were clearing my womb, removing the dead contents. These contents were my first baby, who I never knew existed.

Everything happened so fast that it was only later that it dawned on me that I had conceived and lost a baby. Confusion kicked in, and false guilt followed. Should I have married this man? Is God angry with me? Why me? My emotions took me on a terrible journey and placed a limitation on me as I could not function fully in that mental state. I lost my joy, because I had a thousand questions with no answers. Like Hannah, I cried in anguish. After a long while, much prayer and encouragement, things got better.

The Lord helped me move on, as he healed my broken heart. Two years later we decided it was time to try again for a baby. This was the most daunting task, because I wasn't conceiving. We saw doctor after doctor. They told me my chances were slim due to a type of a hormonal imbalance condition. That was the beginning of years of sorrow and pain of wanting a child, and not having one.

What I could not understand was why many people, who were not married, were conceiving. Some did not even want those babies, why not me? So we started engaging in prayer, fasting, confessing scriptures and all sorts, but no cloud appeared in my horizon!

After a long wait, it finally happened! We were excited and overwhelmed as we discovered I was pregnant. My husband, Osie, was so supportive, and he prayed that all would go well. We celebrated and Osie was spoiling me indeed. We could not wait for the bump to show. As soon as it did, Osie did a massive shopping trip for me, and he was holding my hand as we walked in the malls in Johannesburg. This was his baby, and if the baby was a girl she would be called Dad's Girl – in Zulu 'Ntombikayise' – that's how excited he was. Due to my condition I was scanned regularly, and put under the care of Dr. Ashley Rayman, a very experienced gynaecologist. There was great joy and hope in the Sibanda household because our long awaited for baby was coming.

A month later, I went for my scheduled scan. Osie was not with me because as far as we knew everything was okay, and he had just come back from a night shift so he did not have to come with me. When I saw the doctor's facial expression during the scan,

I knew there was a problem. He repeated the scan about three times. Then he said, "I am sorry, there is no heartbeat."

I had no clue what that meant, so I asked where the heartbeat had gone and what was he going to do to bring it back. He saw that I did not understand, so he put it in layman's terms: "Your baby won't make it." "Has the baby died," I asked? "Is that what you mean?" He nodded his head. My heart sank.

You can imagine the horror of another loss bearing down on me. I was going to go through the same cycle again. I asked him to check again and he confirmed the inevitable. I asked him what's next, and he said I was to go into hospital the next day and they would see what was next. I went back home and threw myself in my husband's arms and started screaming. He knew what had happened.

That night, excruciating pain crippled me. I could not walk, sit or stand. Strong contractions started, followed by bleeding. I was rushed to the hospital and the next day was the end of that pregnancy.

How could this happen again? Was all this pain for nothing? I was very hurt and angry. Like Hannah, I lost my appetite. I would cry uncontrollably. Was God mocking me? Was there any point in praying? Where was God when I was losing my baby? Couldn't He have prevented this? Did He not make heaven and earth? Is there a God up there or are we wasting our time? I was very disappointed and did not want to hear a thing. I felt ashamed, embarrassed and a failure, and did not want to hear about pregnancy ever again! How could I keep on carrying then miss what I was carrying? That was enough!

Time passed, and I received a card from my sister Tracy. She encouraged me with a scripture from *Habakkuk*, of all books! It was *chapter 3:17-19 (NIV)*: *"Though the fig tree does not bud and there are no grapes on the vines, though the olive crop fails and the fields produce no food, though there are no sheep in the pen and no cattle in the stalls, yet I will rejoice in the LORD, I will be joyful in God my Saviour. The Sovereign LORD IS MY STRENGTH; he makes my feet like the feet of a deer, he enables me to tread on the heights."*

It spoke to me greatly and I connected with it. That was the beginning of my healing journey. I learnt that I should not love God for what He gives or love Him when conditions are perfect, but for who He is, the God of my salvation, who is my strength. Needless to say, many believers prayed for me, even though at the beginning I was not open to their encouragement. The Lord took me on a journey and it was a process.

The journey continued and I started studying the life of Hannah. I read about her struggles and I learnt the importance of pouring out my heart to the Lord instead of hardening my heart towards Him. A year later, I was not feeling very well and went to the GP to be examined. He gave me a urine test to see if I was pregnant and it was negative. This did not surprise me because I was not expecting to be pregnant. After all, I had given up hope. I was treated for a urinary tract infection and given antibiotics. However, soon after that I started bleeding heavily and Osie suggested that we consult the gynaecologist. He scanned me and to our absolute shock, and his, there was a little heart beating on the screen. We found out that I was 12 weeks pregnant!

I wondered, "God, are you playing tricks on us? What's this now? Did I ask for a baby?" A thousand thoughts started running through my confused mind. All I remember about that day was my husband touching my belly, declaring, "Not this one! This baby will not die but live to declare the works of the Lord! God is not a man that He should lie." The doctor was very concerned and gave me medication to stop the bleeding, but he said he was not sure about the outcome. I had to be carefully monitored. My husband stood his ground and had faith in God. He summoned for prayer support and the Lord answered. On the 12th of May 1996 (Mother's Day) we were blessed with a bouncy, beautiful baby girl who we named Ayanda MaBlessing, meaning 'our blessings have increased'. What a wonderful mother's day gift from the Lord! There was great joy in Park Lane clinic in Johannesburg. The Lord made us parents. Our lives have never been the same since then. She was such a pleasant gift and she still is. As we held our baby, the peace of God filled our hearts and our sorrows were wiped away.

Sadly, four years after I gave birth to Ayanda, I had another miscarriage. Again, I was not aware that I had conceived because I was told it was an ovarian cyst which would dissolve. After two months I was experiencing a lot of pain and the doctor decided to do keyhole surgery. I was admitted to hospital, and during the procedure they discovered a foetus. I only learnt about my predicament on the following day when the doctor did his morning rounds. I was very frustrated because of what the original diagnosis had been and wondered if my baby could have been saved had it not been mistaken for a cyst. I was very angry and disappointed as a million thoughts were racing through my mind. Could this have been a boy or girl? Who was this baby going to look like? What would have become of this child in life? Could I have done anything differently to save my baby? Why me? This limitation unquestionably affected me. Thank God I had Ayanda. Her presence in my life made the grieving process a little bit lighter as I had to focus on her and not be drowned in my sorrows.

After about three years, Osie and I migrated from South Africa to the United Kingdom. We were Bible school students with very little income and sharing a house with another family. Although it was not a comfortable situation, we were very content with our lives and our daughter. Ayanda was now 6 years old. The thought of having another baby was very far from our minds – as far as the east is from the west!

It was during my final year of Bible school that I started to feel unwell and strong smells were affecting me, especially when I was cooking or when my lecturer would bring coffee into the lecture hall. I thought the coffee was rotten! The situation seemed to get worse and worse. I asked my pastor to pray for me and he casually asked if I was pregnant. I laughed! I thought it was a big joke! I wondered how on earth God could give me another child when we couldn't afford one or when I wasn't even asking Him for another baby. I didn't think Osie was asking the Lord, but maybe Ayanda was as she did often ask for a baby brother or sister. We always blanked her request, knowing the pain it took us just to have her. We would tell her that children come from the Lord and so we had to wait for Him, although in our hearts we were not waiting for any baby.

I reluctantly took a pregnancy test and discovered that I was already 8 weeks pregnant. I experienced many mixed emotions, including sadness and joy. One would think that I should be ecstatic with this news, but I was very aware of our financial situation. Also, unlike having Ayanda in South Africa, I would not have as much help. My parents, in-laws and immediate family were far away, although my brother did live in the same city as me in the UK. However, I could not expect much from him and his wife since they had their own 3 school-going children to look after. Furthermore, they worked full-time.

I wondered why, when the conditions didn't seem perfect to have a baby, the Lord blessed us again. And yet when the conditions seemed perfect to us, it was a struggle to have a child. Perhaps this is what Isaiah meant when he said that God's ways and thoughts are higher than ours *(Isaiah 55:10)*. On the 18th of May 2003 at Southmead Hospital in Bristol, I delivered a healthy baby girl. We named her Realeboga, meaning 'we thank you, Lord, we are grateful to you', and Phumzile, meaning 'rest'.

God has given us rest from all our sorrows associated with conception and we are grateful to Him. We love our daughters dearly. Beyond our struggles and pains are these two beautiful girls. There is a seven-year gap between the two, which means that when Ayanda goes to university we will still have Realeboga at home, and although the whole journey has had tears and pain in between, surely joy came in the morning! *(Psalm 30:5)*

Hannah's journey had pain and sorrow, but joy came. I too suffered, but joy came. If you are going through any painful circumstances, be encouraged, every situation is subject to change. God changes things when we pray. He also changes us and our perspectives of life. God is near to the broken-hearted, and His ear is attentive to their cry. Do not lower God down to the level of your situation; rather lift your situation up to God.

Be real with Him and don't pretend. Don't spiritualise your struggle by trying to impress anyone. Be real to yourself, others and God, because He already knows where you are at. Refuse to be defined by your current situation and allow the Lord and others to help you. Avoid the common tendency to self-blame when things go wrong. Bad things happen to both the good and the bad, just as God *"makes His sun rise on the evil and on the good, and sends rain on the just and on the unjust" (Matthew 5:45).* Struggles of life are not an accurate indication of the spiritual condition of a person. It's not a lack of faith either.

Ever since the fall of mankind, when suffering was introduced, pain has been part of our experience. Sometimes we cause ourselves pain, but God is merciful and comes to help us fix the mess. However, Hannah's case was not self-inflicted, she was barren and we don't know why that was so. I also don't know why I had those miscarriages and I don't seek to know; no one on earth knows why. Don't allow anyone to try and give reasons why you are going through challenges unless it's a clear medical condition. Even then, it is God who has the final say.

Daughter of the Most High God, arise and defy your limitations. Do not allow your circumstances to dictate how far you go in life. You have a story to tell, so don't be silenced. It will work out for your good. Keep going, the Lord is with you.

You do not know who your story is going to encourage. When I went through my ordeal I never dreamt that one day I would be writing and encouraging others. In fact, the Lord has used the limitations Satan wanted to shackle me with to be the source of encouragement for many women. Like Hannah with the birth of Samuel. What satan wanted to achieve was thwarted.

Take courage – it is going to be better. All will be well with you.

Chapter Two

Reflect, Pray and Apply

💬 Reflection points

- What aspects of my story can you identify with?

- Are you facing any emotional challenges?

- How are you dealing with them?

💟 Practical steps to take

1. Find a quiet place and pray.

2. Ask the Lord to heal you of any hurts.

3. Let go of all your disappointments; count your blessings and thank God for them.

📖 Scripture Focus

Romans 8:26-28 (*ESV*)

"Likewise the Spirit helps us in our weakness. For we do not know what to pray for as we ought, but the Spirit intercedes for us with groanings too deep for words. And he who searches hearts knows what is the mind of the Spirit, because the Spirit intercedes for the saints according to the will of God. And we know that for those who love God, all things work together for good, for those who are called according to His purpose."

Proverbs 3:5 (*ESV*)

"Trust in the Lord with all your heart, and do not lean on your own understanding."

It will all work together for your good. You might not understand what you are going through and why you are going through it but trust in the Lord with all your heart and He will see you through.

Chapter Three
Daughter, Your Faith...

The dictionary defines the word 'defy' as to: effectively resist, challenge, frustrate, confront, disregard, ignore, and insult. This is exactly what some women have to do to their limitations in order to maximise their potential. I would like to introduce you to a courageous woman whose account is rendered in the book of *Luke, chapter 8 verse 43-48*:

"And there was a woman who had had a discharge of blood for twelve years, and though she had spent all her living on physicians, she could not be healed by anyone. She came up behind him and touched the fringe of his garment, and immediately her discharge of blood ceased. And Jesus said, "Who was it that touched me?" When all denied it, Peter said, "Master, the crowds surround you

and are pressing in on you!" But Jesus said, "Someone touched me, for I perceive that power has gone out from me." And when the woman saw that she was not hidden, she came trembling, and falling down before him declared in the presence of all the people why she had touched him, and how she had been immediately healed. And he said to her, "Daughter, your faith has made you well; go in peace."

Because of her circumstances she was labelled as 'the woman with the issue of blood'. This condition must have caused her years of tremendous discomfort. Twelve frustrating years in fact; that is 144 months, or 4,380 days, or 105,120 hours to be precise. On average, a woman's monthly menstrual cycle (or period) lasts between three to five days and in some extreme cases it can last for more than seven days. Yet for this woman, one month turned into two, three, four, five... twelve... years...! What woman can endure this condition and not be worn out, restricted, or embarrassed?

Furthermore, monthly periods often don't arrive silently. Many women know that their period is due because they have premenstrual pains. Women experience other discomforts such as acne, bloating, weight gain, nausea, headache, food cravings, irritability, mood swings, crying spells and even depression. All these come from the hormonal changes taking place in their body. I'm sure that as you are reading this, you can identify with at least one, if not more, if you are a woman.

Apart from the 'before' discomforts that accompany a period, a woman also has to deal with the 'during' and sometimes even 'after' discomforts. During her cycle she needs to pay special attention to her hygiene and regularly check herself. Has she spoiled her clothes? Is she giving off undesirable odours? Do her pads or tampons need changing? For some women periods debilitate, leaving them unable to function at all. They may find themselves curled up somewhere, taking anti-inflammatory medication to try and ease the excruciating pain they feel. Now imagine the woman in *Luke 8* who most likely endured some, if not all of these things on a continual basis. Let me emphasise again... for twelve years!

The scriptures don't explain the cause of her condition but what is known is that her bleeding was unusual and abnormally prolonged. Every day she was losing blood and this was dangerous. Blood is vital to life. It provides the body with necessary nutrition, oxygen and waste material removal. It performs various vital functions in the body, including immunological functions, messenger functions, coagulation and regulation of the core body temperature. One can only imagine how many litres of blood this woman lost in twelve years. Whether it was merely menstrual, a severe gynaecological bleeding disorder, or haemorrhaging, the fact remains that in losing so much blood, any of the above vital blood functions might have been affected in her body.

Not only was this woman losing blood, she was also losing money. She had spent all her livelihood trying to find a solution, but no doctor could find a cure. Surely it was demoralising and disappointing to repeatedly hear the same answer from the doctor, "Sorry, there is nothing we can do for you." At that time, there was no such thing as health insurance or a free National Health Service (NHS). If she spent all her livelihood on searching for an answer, how did she live? Perhaps at the mercy of others. Her physical limitation depleted her resources, imposing upon her emotional and psychological frustrations. There was no way she could have functioned to her maximum potential under such conditions.

Not only that, this woman encountered further restrictions placed on her by the Jewish customs of that time. *Leviticus 15:25-27 (ESV)* describes this: *"If a woman has a discharge of blood for many days, not at the time of her menstrual impurity, or if she has a discharge beyond the time of her impurity, all the days of the discharge she shall continue in uncleanness. As in the days of her impurity, she shall be unclean. Every bed on which she lies, all the days of her discharge, shall be to her as the bed of her impurity. And everything on which she sits shall be unclean, as in the uncleanness of her menstrual impurity. And whoever touches these things shall be unclean, and shall wash his clothes and bathe himself in water and be unclean until the evening. But if she is cleansed of her discharge, she shall count for herself seven days, and after that she shall be clean."*

According to this law this woman was very unclean. Not only was she unclean but even the bed she slept on was considered unclean, and any place she sat on was considered unclean. Anyone who touched her bed was unclean and had to wash, and for that whole day that person was unclean. A woman who completed her cycle had to wait seven days before even being considered clean again. Not only that, she could not privately declare herself clean, but had to go to the priest with an offering of two turtledoves or two pigeons and stand at the entrance of the Temple (see *verse 29-30*). The priest would then perform a purification offering with one and a burnt offering with the other. After this exceptionally daunting task the woman would be clean until her next cycle!

In today's world, this whole process could be equated to taking an offering to the priest or pastor every month after a woman has had her period. He would then pray for her, be paid, and declare her clean again. How many women would be comfortable letting their pastor know each time that they were menstruating? It would be an infringement of their privacy! Also, how much money would the pastor make if he had a hundred women in his congregation? One can only imagine.

If that law still applied today, I wonder how many of us would rather hide our periods than be viewed as dirty, impure, vile, defiled, polluted, or filthy, just to name a few synonyms of the word 'unclean'? Yet in her case and according to the law at the time, the woman was considered to be permanently 'dirty' or 'filthy'. Maybe a person could tolerate being unclean for a few days in a month, but to be seen as foul for 4,380 days must have been nerve-wrecking. I don't know how she coped mentally, socially, emotionally, ritually and otherwise! There were definitely multiple limitations prevalent in her life, hence it did not merely rain, it heavily poured!

Despite her traumatising circumstances, this woman was very daring. She wanted to get to Jesus and the Bible says that He faced smothering crowds. Another translation says that the crowds almost crushed Him. She had to push past all the people to get to Him and according to the law every person that touched her became instantly unclean. Just imagine, she was contaminating every single person that touched her or even brushed past her, yet she didn't care. She was fed up with her situation and pushed through the crowd to get to Jesus. Nothing was going to hinder her from getting her breakthrough. She defied all the barriers in front of her. Jesus was her focus and nothing else mattered. She must have heard about Him and the miracles that He performed, otherwise why take such a huge risk? Surely He was the answer that she was searching for.

Luke 8:44 says that, *"She came up behind him and touched the hem of his garment, and at once her bleeding stopped."* This woman physically felt her bleeding stop. She knew what it felt like to have a continual flow and now she was experiencing something totally different. It was only her and Jesus who knew that a secret transaction had taken place at that moment. Although Jesus asked, *"Who touched me?"* He knew exactly who had touched Him and there was a reason for his question. *Verse 45-46 says, "When everyone denied it, Peter said, "Master, the crowds are surrounding you and pressing in on you!" But Jesus said, "Someone touched me. I know that power has gone out from me."* Even the woman was silent at this point, probably unsure of her fate. Perhaps she feared for her life. In *verse 47* it says that, *"When the woman saw that she couldn't escape notice, she came trembling and fell before Jesus. In front of everyone, she explained why she had touched him and how she had been immediately healed. "Daughter, your faith has healed you," Jesus said. "Go in peace."*

Jesus' response was priceless! He called her 'daughter'. She was instantly reinstated into her community where she could now participate with freedom. Jesus had made her who was unclean clean. He made the outcast a daughter. He set the captive free as He promised He would. By touching the hem of His garment, the woman touched His power, and this power was beyond what any physician could offer her.

Jesus knew what courage it took for the woman to do what she did. What an audacious lady! Her faith and hope in Him were not disappointed. By referring to her faith Jesus was not saying that faith itself had creative ability, but that those who put their faith in Him would receive help from Him. Her faith was in who Jesus was and what He could do, not only for others but also for her. What a wonderful ending to years of shame and turmoil. Jesus did a miracle for her, but she also actively participated in it by pushing past all her limitations. She got her breakthrough by getting to Jesus, the ultimate solution provider and terminator of all impossible situations.

Both Hannah and the woman with the issue of blood had physical limitations that caused them emotional mayhem. Their faith in God resulted in their victory and they defied their limitations. Although the strategy for their breakthrough was different, the outcome was that God heard and answered. He removed all that was limiting them. Rest assured He will do the same for you. There is no limiting condition in your life that Jesus cannot handle. There is no label placed on you that He cannot remove. Reach out to Him and He will help you. Have faith in God. The One who was formerly known as a woman with the issue of blood became a daughter. Jesus took away the negative label placed on her and gave her 'beauty for her ashes'.

Chapter Three

Reflect, Pray and Apply

🗩 Reflection points

- What aspects of this woman's life do you identify with?

- What is your understanding of having faith in God?

- Is there any pattern/situation recurring in your life?

🖤 Practical steps to take

1. Reach out to the Lord in prayer.

2. Meditate on God's Word and embrace who He says you are.

3. Have FAITH in Him for He is able to deliver you.

4. If you need counselling, ask for help from your spiritual oversight.

5. If you need medical attention, don't hesitate to go and make an appointment with your GP.

📖Scripture Focus

Hebrews 11:1-6 (*KJV*)

"Now faith is the substance of things hoped for, the evidence of things not seen. For by it the elders obtained a good report. Through faith we understand that the worlds were framed by the word of God, so that things which are seen were not made of things which do appear. By faith Abel offered unto God a more excellent sacrifice than Cain, by which he obtained witness that he was righteous, God testifying of his gifts: and by it he being dead yet speaketh. By faith Enoch was translated that he should not see death; and was not found, because God had translated him: for before his translation he had this testimony, that he pleased God. But without faith it is impossible to please him: for he that cometh to God must believe that he is, and that he is a rewarder of them that diligently seek him."

Mark 11:22 (*NIV*)

"'Have faith in God,' Jesus answered."

1 John 5:14-15 *(ESV)*

"And this is the confidence that we have toward him, that if we ask anything according to his will he hears us. And if we know that he hears us in whatever we ask, we know that we have the requests that we have asked of him."

Isaiah 61:1-4 *(NKJV)*

The Spirit of the Lord God is upon me, because the Lord has anointed me to bring good news to the poor; he has sent me to bind up the brokenhearted, to proclaim liberty to the captives, and the opening of the prison to those who are bound; to proclaim the year of the Lord's favor, and the day of vengeance of our God; to comfort all who mourn; to grant to those who mourn in Zion — to give them a beautiful headdress instead of ashes, the oil of gladness instead of mourning, the garment of praise instead of a faint spirit; that they may be called oaks of righteousness, the planting of the Lord, that he may be glorified. They shall build up the ancient ruins; they shall raise up the former devastations; they shall repair the ruined cities, the devastations of many generations.

Chapter Four
Diligent Dorcas

The word 'diligent' denotes consistency in effort to accomplish something. It also means persevering and hard-working. Some of its synonyms include being active, attentive, steadfast, unrelenting, industrious, untiring and laborious. All these words are an accurate description of Dorcas, the woman we are introduced to in *Acts 9:36-42 (ESV)*: *"Now there was in Joppa a disciple named Tabitha, which, translated, means Dorcas. She was full of good works and acts of charity. In those days she became ill and died, and when they had washed her, they laid her in an upper room. Since Lydda was near Joppa, the disciples, hearing that Peter was there, sent two men to him, urging him, "Please come to us without delay." So Peter rose and went with them. And when he arrived, they took him to the upper room. All the widows stood beside him weeping and showing tunics and other garments that Dorcas made while she was with them. But Peter put them all outside, and knelt down and prayed; and turning to the body he said, "Tabitha, arise." And she opened her eyes, and when she saw Peter she sat up. And he gave her his hand and raised her up. Then calling the saints and widows, he presented her alive. And it became known throughout all Joppa, and many believed in the Lord."*

Dorcas was a pleasant woman who was strategically positioned at a seaport town, which is believed to have been the place where the prophet Jonah took off to Tarshish instead of Nineveh. There was a growing Christian population in that area and this might have been how Dorcas heard the Gospel.

The opening statement of *verse 36* introduces Dorcas as a disciple. The word disciple means a person who is an adherent of the doctrine of another. It also means a follower, a learner, a believer or a pupil. This shows that Dorcas had embraced the faith and she was an adherent follower of the teachings of Christ and the Apostles. She embraced the faith, and was both a believer and a pupil. She applied what she was taught. This is confirmed by scripture when it says that she was a woman who was full of good works. To be full of good works implies being industrious and not idle. The word 'full' also indicates that her life was purposefully and intentionally filled with an abundance of good. She was a practical woman and didn't just verbalise her faith. She demonstrated it. Her faith in God was used for the purpose of serving her community and not for selfish gain. She had no limitations in serving.

Dorcas was compassionate, committed and consistent. Her good deeds were not targeted at those who could give back to her because the recipients of her ministry were the poor and widowed who relied on her generosity. She did charitable deeds out of a charitable heart. She was a definite asset to her community and was an investor in people. She was a significant woman who developed good relationships with the people around her. In order to know their needs, she must have been close to them. She was relevant to the world she lived in. Her faith in God made her secure. You can only love others to the degree you love yourself, and you can only love yourself truly if you are secure in God.

As the story of Dorcas unfolds, we learn that she became sick. This sickness became a limitation to her good works. The Bible doesn't give any specifics about her illness but it does say that the sickness eventually led to her death. All her usefulness was taken from her. Death put an end to her purposeful ministry to her community. She was robbed of her ability to bless others. All her impact and daily assignments were stopped. Her death brought everything to a standstill. Her light, which was shining so brightly, was switched off.

Here is a woman who impacted her community by her good works, she was diligent, loving and caring, but now lay dead because of an illness. Dorcas was described as a devout follower of Jesus, and yet she still fell ill. She was a pillar and a role model, the true epitome of a godly woman, so what went wrong? Did she not exercise her faith? Did she not know the healing scriptures? Did she confess negatively and bring this on herself? Why would a woman full of good works suffer illness and fail to recover? Did she commit sin somewhere or was this a generational curse following her from her bloodline? Why Dorcas, of all women? Was there not a better candidate for illness in Joppa among the disobedient ones?

All these questions are asked today when calamity strikes a person of faith and good works. Sadly, we do not always have the answers, even though we would like to believe we do. Being a godly or devout Christian does not exempt anyone from suffering. God remains sovereign through it all and is a safe refuge to all who run to him *(Proverbs 18:10)* He promised never to leave or forsake any of His children.

I can imagine how the news of Dorcas' death was received by those who were beneficiaries of her kindness. It must have deeply shattered and devastated them, because she was so motherly and caring towards them. How could this happen after she had done so much good for them? Her death must have brought her community to a standstill, but they refused to let her go. Being believers, they knew she had gone to be with the Lord. Although they may have prayed for her themselves, they knew they needed a miracle. Therefore they summoned Peter to come and help them. They knew that Peter had performed a miracle before so there was hope for them.

When Peter arrived, he was taken to the room where Dorcas lay, and an interesting scenario unfolded. All the widows – not some but all – stood around him. They were all crying, showing the deep loss and pain they were in. As they wept bitterly, they were showing Peter her good works through the garments, robes and other clothes she handmade for them. Peter asked to be left alone with her. Then he knelt down, as a sign of his humility, respect and dependency on God. He prayed to God for this limitation to be removed. *"Turning toward the dead woman, he said, "Tabitha, get up." She opened her eyes, and seeing Peter she sat up. He took her by the hand and helped her to her feet. Then he called for the believers, especially the widows, and presented her to them alive"* (Acts 9:40-41).

There must have been great rejoicing to see Dorcas alive once again. I can see the people clapping their hands and dancing or simply crying for joy. God had removed the barrier. The limitation had been defied. This news became known all over Joppa. Today's headlines would read: "DEAD DORCAS' DEEDS DEFY DEATH". We know it is the Lord who brought her back to life when Peter prayed for her. However, her deeds were the catalyst that triggered the action that her community took. If Dorcas was full of bad works and was mean to the people, I don't think her story would have had the same ending.

Unlike the current tendencies of screaming and shouting seen in some television 'miracle workers', Peter simply prayed and then told Dorcas to rise up. In order to do this, Peter was led by the Holy Spirit. It would be unwise to think that anybody can just call a person back to life. If this was so, the mortuaries would be empty today. Be careful not to be deceived by those who claim certain spiritual powers to bring the dead back to life as so many people have been disillusioned when their loved ones were not resurrected!

As Joppa was a sea port it is likely that this news travelled beyond Joppa. People must have told their relatives far and wide about this amazing event that had taken place. Many people believed in the Lord as a result of her resurrection. Her influence was no doubt amplified by her coming back to life. The seeds of love and care which she had sown in others spoke for her in her time of need. The people she invested in witnessed for her when she had been silenced by death. Her activities of compassion became her voice.

How we treat others matters in life. Defying limitations is not so that we can enjoy victory alone. It is our weapon for helping others who might be going through hardship. Our faith in God is not just for securing us a mansion in heaven, but it's also for standing in the gap for the welfare of others. Like Dorcas, our faith must be accompanied by good works, regardless of what we are going through. *James 2:14-18 (NIV)* says this about faith and good works: *"What good is it, my brothers and sisters, if someone claims to have faith but has no deeds? Can such faith save them? Suppose a brother or a sister is without clothes and daily food. If one of you says to them, "Go in peace; keep warm and well fed," but does nothing about their physical needs, what good is it? In the same way, faith by itself, if it is not accompanied by action, is dead. But someone will say, "You have faith; I have deeds." Show me your faith without deeds, and I will show you my faith by my deeds."*

Needless to say, our good works do not secure us a place in heaven. Jesus Christ has already paid the price for our salvation. We do good works because the good One resides in us, and because the Lord Jesus, our example, went about doing good *(Acts 10:38)*. As his disciples, we should follow his steps.

Like Hannah, it was through prayer that the limitations placed on Dorcas were defied. Like the woman with the issue of blood, faith in God had to be exercised. In my case, it was our prayers, the prayers of others, having faith in God, and refusing to accept the report of doctors that day. You too, can defy your limitation. Your strategy may be different from mine, or the others previously mentioned, but rest assured that God will answer you. Don't give up. The story of your life will end well. God has good plans for you and He loves you dearly. Continue to be diligent in loving and serving Him. God is a rewarder of those who diligently seek Him *(Hebrews 11:6)*.

Chapter Four

Reflect, Pray and Apply

💬 Reflection points

- Like Dorcas, are you a disciple of Jesus?

- Do you have both faith and good works evident in your life?

- Can you list some of your good works and who is benefitting from them?

- Are you leaving a godly legacy for others?

- What is currently limiting your spiritual growth and subsequent good works?

💗 Practical steps to take

1. Pray, asking the Lord to help you to be a good disciple.

2. Evaluate your life and identify the areas where you might not have been applying His Word, and repent.

3. Begin to be a blessing to others. Deliberately choose someone to bless with what you have.

4. Determine to live a lifestyle of kindness.

📖Scripture Focus

1 Corinthians 13:1-13 *(ESV)*

"If I speak in the tongues of men and of angels, but have not love, I am a noisy gong or a clanging cymbal. And if I have prophetic powers, and understand all mysteries and all knowledge, and if I have all faith, so as to remove mountains, but have not love, I am nothing. If I give away all I have, and if I deliver up my body to be burned, but have not love, I gain nothing. Love is patient and kind; love does not envy or boast; it is not arrogant or rude. It does not insist on its own way; it is not irritable or resentful; it does not rejoice at wrongdoing, but rejoices with the truth. Love bears all things, believes all things, hopes all things, endures all things. Love never ends. As for prophecies, they will pass away; as for tongues, they will cease; as for knowledge, it will pass away. For we know in part and we prophesy in part, but when the perfect comes, the partial will pass away. When I was a child, I spoke like a child, I thought like a child, I reasoned like a child. When I became a man, I gave up childish ways. For now we see in a mirror dimly, but then face to face. Now I know in part; then I shall know fully, even as I have been fully known. So now faith, hope, and love abide, these three; but the greatest of these is love."

Romans 12:9-21 (*ESV*)

"Let love be genuine. Abhor what is evil; hold fast to what is good. Love one another with brotherly affection. Outdo one another in showing honour. Do not be slothful in zeal, be fervent in spirit, serve the Lord. Rejoice in hope, be patient in tribulation, be constant in prayer. Contribute to the needs of the saints and seek to show hospitality. Bless those who persecute you; bless and do not curse them. Rejoice with those who rejoice, weep with those who weep. Live in harmony with one another. Do not be haughty, but associate with the lowly. Never be wise in your own sight. Repay no one evil for evil, but give thought to do what is honourable in the sight of all. If possible, so far as it depends on you, live peaceably with all. Beloved, never avenge yourselves, but leave it to the wrath of God, for it is written, 'Vengeance is mine, I will repay, says the Lord.' To the contrary, 'if your enemy is hungry, feed him; if he is thirsty, give him something to drink; for by so doing you will heap burning coals on his head.' Do not be overcome by evil, but overcome evil with good."

Chapter Five
Have Mercy on Me, Oh Lord!

L
et us explore an interesting account found in
Matthew chapter 15 verses 22-28. This is the
story of a woman whose limitation was due to
her Gentile background and her daughter's illness.

*"A Canaanite woman from that vicinity came to him,
crying out, 'Lord, Son of David, have mercy on me!
My daughter is demon-possessed and suffering terribly.'
Jesus did not answer a word. So his disciples came to him
and urged him, 'Send her away, for she keeps crying out
after us.' He answered, 'I was sent only to the lost sheep
of Israel.' The woman came and knelt before him. 'Lord,
help me!' she said. He replied, 'It is not right to take the
children's bread and toss it to the dogs.' 'Yes it is, Lord,'
she said. 'Even the dogs eat the crumbs that fall from their
master's table.' Then Jesus said to her, 'Woman, you have*

great faith! Your request is granted.' And her daughter was healed at that moment." (NIV)

A Canaanite was viewed as a pagan, undeserving of the promises of God, which were solely the privilege of Israelites (Jews). Canaanites were also viewed as ancient enemies of God's people and could therefore not claim access to any benefits bestowed on Jews. The Canaanite woman was a Gentile and during her time, Gentiles were despised and considered to be no better than dogs. Having this type of background naturally disqualified her from requesting anything from Jesus. Her condition did not stop her because she was desperate for help and she was determined to get it.

The situation distressing this woman was not something directly in her own life, but her daughter who, the Bible says, was grievously vexed by an evil spirit. This means that a satanic force and principality was controlling, dominating, harassing and tossing her daughter about. Simply put, her daughter was possessed. Demons were residing in her, causing her to do strange and abnormal things. As a mother, witnessing the misery of her demon-possessed daughter was devastating and ripping her heart apart.

The Bible teaches that children are a heritage from the Lord *(Psalm 127:3-5)*, so whether Canaanite or not, this woman's child was from the Lord and yet had been taken over by a demon. Both her and her daughter were helpless. It was a spiritual issue that needed a spiritual answer. She had to do something about it. She did not wallow in a 'woe is me' attitude of self-pity but rather believed that there had to be a solution to her daughter's terrible situation. She was fed up of watching demons oppress her loved one, so she rose up against the odds. Her crisis didn't defeat her; instead it became a catalyst for her determination to find a solution. In a daring move, she approached Jesus for mercy.

Initially, the response she received from Him wasn't desirable. He seemed to focus on the fact that she was a Canaanite and did not qualify for the 'bread' (in this case, healing) which was meant for the children. But the woman did not sulk or give up; she knew Jesus could help because He had done it before. It didn't matter what name she was called in the process of getting a breakthrough for her daughter, what mattered to her was being helped. She persisted in asking for mercy from the merciful Saviour. She knew she didn't deserve it, but she believed that mercy could override any condition.

She said, "even dogs get crumbs from their owners." She meant, "I might be seen as a dog, but I still need mercy, You are the Deliverer, and You can deliver my daughter."

"Then Jesus said to her, 'Woman, you have great faith! Your request is granted.' And her daughter was healed at that moment" (Matthew 15:28, NIV). Mercy spoke for her. Mercy said 'no more!' to the demonic possession.

Under normal circumstances, things that affect our families tend to affect us as well. Although your limitation might not be something in your own life, it will still have a bearing on you. Be it a husband or a sibling or any close relative being harassed by demons, one way or the other. It could be a rebellious child, a cheating or abusive husband, an irresponsible mother, a spiteful in-law, or a jealous sibling. It could also be a controlling spiritual or natural parent, a selfish aunt, a proud uncle, maybe even a nephew on drugs, a short-tempered niece or an alcoholic step-father... the list is endless. All these situations can depress you if not managed well. Because they are an indicator of the powers of darkness operating in an individual's life, only prayer can help. Mercy can also speak for you as the woman with her daughter experienced! Cry out to God for mercy on their behalf.

I vividly remember Easter Sunday in April 2009 when I went to see my dad who had visited the UK. He was living in Warwick with my brother and his family. I had spoken to him, letting him know we were going to visit him so he could spend time with his grandchildren. My daughters, Ayanda and Lebo, were so keen to go and spend time with him. Ayanda had won medals at a student's convention and was eager to go and show her granddad.

When we got to Warwick we were very excited. We are always excited when we go to visit my brother and having dad there was even a bonus. When we got there, I called out from the entrance announcing our arrival. The response was unusually sullen. Prisca, my niece, came to meet us at the door. We greeted her then I asked for my dad. Shockingly, we learnt that he had been rushed to the hospital in an ambulance and was unconscious, suspected to have had either a stroke or a heart attack. Whatever the cause, this was a life-threatening condition. We immediately followed to the hospital.

When we got to the there, I asked the lady at the reception desk, "Excuse me, where is my father?" Puzzled by this question the lady asked who my father was. I found this annoying and I said, "He just came in now. His name is Frederick Chimkupete. Just tell me where he is." We were escorted to the emergency room where my dad lay on a bed in a room with machines and tubes and a heavy presence of medical staff. I could see that whatever his condition, it was very serious. Nurses were whispering around him, checking his pulse and eyes constantly. The heart monitor was beeping and oscillating as you see on movies. When there is a straight line you know the person is dead. My sister-in-law was crying hopelessly and I found my nephew sitting in a room on a corner resigned to hear the obvious.

"Excuse me, what is going on? Can someone tell me what is wrong with my father?" I asked the team. They tried to explain the condition and to let me know that chances are he won't make it. I called my dad and touched him. There was no response. I had never seen my dad motionless before. He lay there silently and appeared to be on his way out. Doctors seemed to have resigned to the fact that he was going to die any minute. Someone offered a cup of tea. In my heart I thought, "Do you want that tea poured on your face? My father is dying and you want me to drink tea!" Of course, she was being kind, but that was not the time for tea to me. I was too much in shock for that.

I continued calling my dad, holding onto his hand but he was not responding. All my siblings had not yet arrived, not to mention those who were overseas. I thought he shouldn't die here. This is not home. So I started telling him he wasn't home, he should fight and rather die at home. I behaved worse than a mad woman. The team saw drama! My husband was helplessly watching.

I started to pray loudly. I did not care about the medical team or being politically correct. I asked God for a miracle. I confessed the healing scriptures I knew, reminding God that this was resurrection Sunday, so He should resurrect my dad. In between I would be calling my dad and there was no response. After a while, I believe the Holy Spirit led me to ask for mercy. So I changed my manner of prayer and just simply asked God to have mercy on me, a sinner. Tears started to roll down my face as I begged for mercy, not only for me, but for my dad, for us, his eight children, for his 16 grandchildren.

I knew if my dad died in the UK it was going to be a double tragedy, not just because he was the only parent we had, but that he would have to go back to Africa in a flight as cargo whilst we go as accompanying passengers and yet he had come to visit us, needless to say the financial implications of transporting a corpse, hence the cry for mercy.

To cut a long story short, God responded to the cry of mercy. God had mercy on us as a family and my dad regained consciousness. His progress defied what the medical team anticipated. Although my dad spent weeks in hospital, he recovered until he was well enough to fly back home.

As my brother escorted him we waved goodbye and cried because we knew that was his last wave. The next time it would be us waving goodbye but he would not be able to wave back. Tears streamed on our faces but we were grateful for mercy. The mercy that stepped into that room and gave us a chance to spend more time with our dad and allowed him to go home safely.

On the 7th of June 2009, my dad slipped away and went to join my mum and the rest of our loved ones who are with the Lord. Dad's death was a painful experience as we became orphans. When we flew for my dad's funeral I was weeping in gratitude that he was not in the cargo section of the flight. Indeed God had mercy on us.

If there are any family situations vexing you, don't give up. We have a merciful God who is able to save.

It might not seem like God is hearing. It might seem like the heavens are closed to you, but don't lose heart. Indeed He will come through for you. Every situation on earth is subject to change. You need to develop the tenacity of a bulldog. Don't let go. Pray until you get your breakthrough, for it will surely happen. Have faith in God. You need to also know that you have a helper, the Holy Spirit, who is ready to assist you and give you the grace while waiting for your answer. Remember that with God, all things are possible *(Matthew 19:26)*. The God who had mercy on us will be merciful to you too.

Chapter Five

Reflect, Pray and Apply

Reflection points

- In which area do you need God's mercy?

- Are you facing any family challenges?

- Have you faced any discrimination?

- Have you lost hope?

- Do you persist in prayer?

- Are you familiar with the person and work of the Holy Spirit?

Practical steps to take

1. Take time to pray about the points you have reflected on. Ask God for mercy.

2. Find a faithful friend to pray with regularly, so you may be encouraged.

3. If you are still struggling with issues, go and talk to your counsellor, mentor, pastor or priest. Get help – don't be silent.

Scripture Focus

Lamentations 3:21-23 *(NKJV)*

"This I recall to my mind, therefore I have hope. Through the Lord's mercies we are not consumed, because His compassions fail not. They are new every morning; Great is Your faithfulness."

Psalm 136:1 *(NKJV)*

"Oh, give thanks to the Lord, for He is good! For His mercy endures forever."

Psalm 103:4,8 *(NKJV)*

"Who redeems your life from destruction, who crowns you with lovingkindness and tender mercies... The Lord is merciful and gracious, slow to anger, and abounding in mercy."

Jeremiah 29:11 *(NKJV)*

"For I know the thoughts that I think toward you, says the LORD, thoughts of peace and not of evil, to give you a future and a hope."

Jeremiah 33:3 (*GNB*)

"'Call to me, and I will answer you; I will tell you wonderful and marvellous things that you know nothing about.'"

Psalm 46 (*NKJV*)

"God is our refuge and strength, a very present help in trouble. Therefore we will not fear, even though the earth be removed, and though the mountains be carried into the midst of the sea; though its waters roar and be troubled, though the mountains shake with its swelling. There is a river whose streams shall make glad the city of God, the holy place of the tabernacle of the Most High. God is in the midst of her, she shall not be moved; God shall help her, just at the break of dawn. The nations raged, the kingdoms were moved; He uttered His voice, the earth melted. The Lord of hosts is with us; the God of Jacob is our refuge. Come, behold the works of the LORD, who has made desolations in the earth. He makes wars cease to the end of the earth; He breaks the bow and cuts the spear in two; He burns the chariot in the fire. Be still, and know that I am God; I will be exalted among the nations, I will be exalted in the earth! The LORD of hosts is with us; the God of Jacob is our refuge."

Conclusion
Daughter Arise! You have what it takes!

Perhaps you have gone through or are currently going through painful circumstances similar to the ones discussed in this book. Maybe you identified with Hannah, the woman with the issue of blood, Dorcas, the Canaanite woman or even me. Or maybe your situation is completely different and it is causing you tremendous pain and tears. I want you to know that there is hope for you.

There is nothing that you are facing or will ever face that is bigger than God. The season of pain is never permanent in life. *"Weeping may endure for a night, but joy comes in the morning" (Psalm 30:5, NKJV)*. Morning does not necessarily mean the next morning, although in some cases it does. It simply means that the season of pain will end.

When you learn to respond appropriately to the season of pain, the fruit of that season will be sweet. Whatever you are going through and whatever you will go through has been experienced by someone before, and they have conquered it. You too will overcome because the Lord is a refuge and shelter for all who have faith in Him. Jesus is a shield and buckler, and defender of the weak. The Redeemer rescues those who run to Him for help, and He is a deliverer and champion of restoration. The Messiah lifts up the despised and levels the ground for them. This applies to you too. What Jesus did for me and the women mentioned in this book, He can do for you. He is able and there is a testimony waiting for you.

You are not what your situation suggests you are; you are who God says you are – His beloved daughter. For every mountain you will face there is a divine strategy to bring you over. Develop your prayer life and learn to hide in God. Continuously empty your heart before the Lord so that you do not became bitter as a result of the pain you may be enduring. Ask for help from the Lord and those who spiritually watch over you, and when you are wrong, repent and apologise as this will only serve to strengthen you. Read and meditate on the scriptures so that you are not deceived by Satan's lies. He may try to blame you for what you are going through or accuse you of not having enough faith. Don't believe him!

Woman, don't allow your limitations to crush you. With God's help you can rise up and defy them all. Higher ground is waiting for you. This is your year of enlargement. God wants to make a difference in your life so that you can make a difference in the lives of others. Join me and thousands of women who have embraced their purpose and have decided to go for all God has for them. Join the army of unstoppable women around the globe who are not succumbing to the pressures of life, but are being used by God to bless their generation. Your place is vacant, so rise up and occupy it, for you have what it takes!

The Lord will surely help you and you will not be hindered anymore.

Therefore, daughter, ARISE! Defy your limitations and scale the utmost height!

Dear friend...

God loves you so much that He gave His only Son, Jesus, so that if you believe in Him you will not perish but have everlasting life. He is the only way to an eternal relationship with God. The choice of where to spend eternity is made here on earth while you are still alive.

I encourage you to give your life to Jesus. You cannot defy your limitations without God. You need to be reconciled back to Him who is the source of everything. Maybe there have been things in your life that have tried to place limitations on you. Be encouraged, God is not finished with you therefore there is hope for you.

Perhaps you don't know how to pray and yet you would like to consider this matter. Here is a prayer to assist you.

Heavenly Father,

I thank You for loving me and sending Your Son to die for my sins. According to Your Word, I confess with my mouth that Jesus is Lord and I believe in my heart that You raised him from the dead so that I may be saved. I invite You to be my Lord and personal Saviour. Forgive me of my sins. I receive the power to become Your child. Your Word says if I call upon Your name I will be saved. I call upon Your name and I know You have saved me now. Amen.

Signed: ....

Dated: ....

Scripture References:
John 3:16; Romans 10:9-13; John 1:12

Tribute to My Family

To my husband, best friend, prayer partner, pastor, work colleague and father of our two lovely daughters, you have been my greatest way-maker. You always raise the stakes for me and help me reach them. I have learnt a lot from your work ethic and from your fatherly heart. My life with you has been an awesome journey. Thank you for believing in me and for not placing any limitations on me as a woman in ministry. You always make room for me to use my gifts without being threatened by them. I may not always like it, but thank you for also correcting me when I do wrong. Twenty-two years later, I'm still in love with you! May the Lord grant you the desires of your heart.

Ayanda and Realeboga, my life would not be the same without you. Ayanda, from the day you were born, I knew there was something special about you. You have grown into this lovely lady with an amazing voice and a passion for music. May you sing songs that will bring hope to the nations. I know you will excel in life because God's hand is on you and you are diligent with your studies. I love you dearly and pray that the Lord will continue to make you the head and not the tail. You were born to make a difference.

Lebo, my dancing queen and drummer, you are very caring and affectionate. You always put your heart in what you do. May your dance bring honour to the Lord. May your drumming usher people into praising God. You too will excel in life because the hand of the Lord is on you. You work hard at school and you do your best. I love you dearly and I pray that your life will be a great influence to your generation.

Thank you my precious daughters for all you are and all you do to inspire and encourage Mummy. Rest assured that no one will ever take your places.

Loulita, you are a God-sent daughter. We have walked together for years and I have seen you being single, married, and now an amazing mum! You first walked in our door as a stranger and now you have become an integral part of our family; this can only be God's doing, and it is marvellous in our eyes. Thank you for all your love and support, and you indeed are an outstanding helper of destiny. We have laughed and cried together and been to places far and wide, and you make things happen. You are an amazing, God-fearing woman and I love you very much. I pray that you become all that God has intended you to be. The best is still to come.

Ade, you are such an interesting daughter, full of life and expression. You are always sincere in what you do. I thank God for your life and for making you a part of our family. Although the circumstances that brought you to our doorstep were not pleasant, the outcome has been more than pleasant. Look what you have become! Thank you for coming right on time to help with this book. You thought you were just coming to work. Look what the Lord has done! May you continue to be led by the Spirit. I love you very much and I know God has great plans for you.

To my family, Prisca, Lilian, Peter and Kudzai, Constance, Tracy and Khopolo, Serviria and Jasper, and last but not least, Joyce, I could not wish for a better family than you. You are all special to me and I have a unique relationship with each one of you. Thank you for loving me and believing in me. You are always there for me and I love you all. God bless you and grant you the desires of your hearts.

Bessie, Kuziva, Tariro, Tsungie, Prisca, Tinashe, Anesu, Tapiwa, Betty, Tawanda, Unalerona, Rebokile, Zvikomborero and Simbarashe, you are all special nieces and nephews to me, and I pray that you may all walk in the ways of the Lord and go on to accomplish great things in life. Chido, Matsatse, Mikaela and Emmanuel, know that Gogo Fatie loves you and God has special plans for you.

To Gogo Alice Sibanda, I have met few women like you. You are the most amazing mother-in-law I have ever seen. You embraced me as your daughter and you are genuine in all you do. I pray that the Lord will continue to strengthen you even in this sunset season of your life. Special thanks to all my in-laws for your love and care.

I thank God for my late parents Frederick and Bessie, for the way I was raised and the principles I was taught, for their love and care and their academic investment in me. They were the vessels God chose to give me the foundation on which my life is built. I will always be grateful.

May they continue to rest in peace till we meet in Gloryland.

Acknowledgements

The scriptures have rightly said, *"Two are better than one, because they have a good reward for their labour"* (KJV), and so is the case with this book. There have been more than two people working alongside me and I thank God for all of you.

While God inspired it all, some have encouraged, edited, cheered on, checked on my progress and proof-read. Without all of these, we wouldn't have this book.

In different stages, seasons and assignments of our lives, God always sends us people to come alongside and help us; our way-makers, or helpers of destiny. These people believe in us and they are committed to seeing our dreams come true. They push us to pursue those dreams and they rejoice with us when those dreams come true. They see potential in us and help us to maximise that potential. I am so grateful to the Lord for all of you.

To Eric and Marcia, thank you for all your support in this project.

To Lois, thank you for further editing and for your continual support.

To Edith and Emmanuel, you are always there for us. Thank you for all the encouragement and support with all our projects.

Pastor Agu and Sola Irukwu, thank you for your encouragement and support.

Pastor Eric and Uba, you are a great inspiration, thank you!

To our church family, you are an amazing congregation and we thank God for blessing us with such loving people. I pray that the Lord will indeed cause us to work together side by side, serving Him with gladness. May He grant you all the desires of your heart and above all, when our life on earth is over, may we all make it to Heaven.

To Hope For Every Woman, partners and friends, thank you for what you are doing to inspire women globally. The Lord will reward you for your diligence, and indeed there is hope for every woman under the sun, and that hope is in Jesus.

Above everyone and everything in the heavens and earth, I'm grateful to the one and only wise God. To my Saviour and King, the source and owner of everything, thank You. To You be all the glory and honour and praise. Without You I am nothing, and this book would not exist. All this is for You. May this book be used for Your glory.

Fatima

Other books from
Sibanda Publishing

ISBN: 978-0-9561175-0-2

The Fragrance of a Godly Woman
by Fatima Sibanda

Woman! You are God's special gift to the world. Deposited within you is a unique and valuable fragrance waiting to be released. Regardless of how you started in life, the experiences you have been through or the challenges you may be currently facing, God has great plans for you. Don't allow anything or anyone to reduce you to something God never intended you to be. This book will equip and empower you to let go of your past, walk in your present and embrace your future. You can rise up, release your godly fragrance and make a difference in this world!

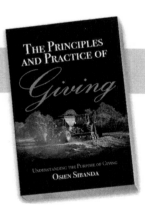

ISBN: 978-0-9561175-1-9

The Principles and Practice of Giving
by Osien Sibanda

Giving is a principle that was established by God for all people to obey. It reflects and demonstrates His loving nature towards people. The motivation of giving should be love and compassion for humanity. The focus of giving is for the benefit of the recipient, not the giver. The concept of giving has been greatly misunderstood in many arenas and has been used as a bait for attracting wealth at the expense of people's ignorance and desire to prosper. This book will help you rediscover the purpose of giving as God intended.

ISBN: 978-0-9561175-2-6

The God Told Me Syndrome
by Osien Sibanda

When someone's introduction to a statement, answer to a question or reason for making a certain decision is, 'God told me...', what should our response be? How do we know that what they are saying is indeed from God? The 'God told me...' or 'God says...' phrase has been grossly misused such that Osien Sibanda describes it as a syndrome. We should not believe what someone says just because they claim God said it. This book will help you to discern when God is really speaking and when He's not.

ISBN: 978-0-9561175-3-3

Count the Cost
by Osien Sibanda

Life is a journey consisting of decisions to be made every step of the way. These have a potential to produce positive or negative outcomes. Count the Cost encourages people to weigh out the long term implications of each and every decision. Some ideas may seem attractive in the short-term, yet in the long run have devastating consequences.
Through its many examples, this book exposes the heavy prices paid by those who did not make wise choices. It is basically a call to count the cost before taking any action.

SIBANDA
PUBLISHING

For more information please contact
info@sibandapublishing.com